D1551165

Dad Facts

Totally Nutritious Information

by
Harry Bright & Jakob Anser

Illustrations by
Michael Halbert

Bright Hart Books
Libertyville, Illinois

ßB

Published by Bright Hart Books
Libertyville, IL 60048

Dad Facts

LC Control Number: 2020931808

ISBN 978-1-950355-03-7

For special orders, quantity sales, or corporate sales, please email
orders@brighthartbooks.com. For trade and wholesale sales, please call
Independent Publishers Group at 1-800-888-4741.

Manufactured in the United States of America

VP 10 9 8 7 6 5 4 3 2 1

Dad Facts

Thanks, Dad. Humans inherit slightly more genetic information from our mother (her DNA plus her mitochondrial DNA), but we *use* about 10 percent more of the DNA received from our father. So, genetically speaking, each of us resembles our father more than our mother.

Rock out with your socks out. The world's oldest pair of socks—stitched together in Egypt sometime between 250 and 420 CE—are bright red, made of wool, and split-toed, proving once and for all that socks were indeed made to be worn with sandals.

When playing footsie gets you to second base. An article in *Dermatology Online Journal* details the case of a twenty-two-year-old Brazilian woman who made medical history by having a category five pseudomamma—an extra nipple with an areola—on the bottom of her foot.

The pen is mightier than the swordsman. Famed American writer Kurt Vonnegut Jr. was briefly Geraldo Rivera's father-in-law, although the marriage between artist Edith Vonnegut and the philandering Rivera ended in acrimony. Ever the protective patriarch, Vonnegut exacted his revenge—on the page. The characters Jerry Rivers and Jerry Cha-cha Rivera appear in several Vonnegut books, and never in a flattering light.

My hero! According to the Strauss–Howe generational theory, America experiences a crisis that destroys the old order and creates a new one every eighty years. Born between 1982 and 2004, millennials—a term coined by William Strauss and Neil Howe—are the latest "Hero" generation, and it is their destiny to lead us until around 2075.

That's a lotta duck face. It is predicted that millennials will snap more than 25,000 selfies in their lifetime.

Nearly half of millennials say they would prefer to live in a socialist country versus a capitalist country. Seven percent say they'd prefer to live under communism. And two-thirds don't know what happened at Auschwitz.

Pics, or it didn't happen. More photographs were taken in 2015 than in the entire preceding history of photography.

Collectively, YouTube users watch eighty years of video every minute.

Dead-end friends. Facebook has around 120 million fake users—that's roughly 1.6 percent of Earth's population.

OK iGenner? The generation after millennials—or "iGen," as psychologist Jean M. Twenge has termed it—feels lonelier and less happy the more time they spend in front of screens. According to Twenge, iGenners who are heavy users of social media increase their risk of depression by 27 percent, and those who spend three hours a day on electronic devices have a 35 percent higher risk for suicide.

Dripping with irony. Ohio businessman Clarence Crane created Life Savers candy in 1912. Two decades later, his son—the poet Hart Crane—drowned when he jumped off an ocean liner.

Keeping up with the Kardashians. More Americans have married Kim Kardashian (three) than have died from Ebola virus disease (two).

Before 1900, the average person consumed no more information throughout their lifetime than what's in a typical Sunday *New York Times*.

A Catholic priest came up with the Big Bang theory. Georges Lemaître, a professor of physics and astronomy at the Catholic University of Leuven, in Belgium, published his "hypothesis of the primeval atom" in the science journal *Nature* in 1931.

In the beginning . . . Fred Hoyle, an atheist astronomer, coined the phrase *Big Bang* during a 1949 radio interview to mock the idea that the universe had a beginning. Hoyle rejected the implication of a causal agent (i.e., God), instead proposing the theory of a steady universe with no beginning or end—a view that has since fallen out of favor.

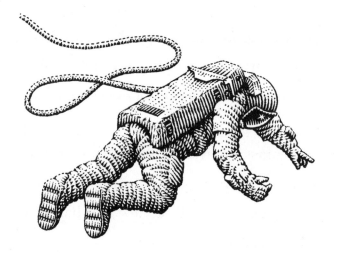

You can't burp in space—not like on Earth, anyway. To separate gas from the liquid in your stomach, earthly gravity is required. Astronauts refer to zero-gravity regurgitative wet burps as *bomit*.

It is theoretically possible to travel faster than the speed of light without actually moving. In 1994, the physicist Miguel Alcubierre proposed a warp drive—a concept first popularized on the TV series *Star Trek*—that would expand the fabric of space behind a ship and shrink it in front, thus allowing the craft to essentially surf down a space-time bubble while remaining motionless. Firing up this warp drive, physicists estimate, would require a hell of a lot of energy: using Einstein's $E=mc^2$, m would have to equal the mass of Jupiter (that's 318 Earths!).

Googolperplexed! The words *googol* (the numeral one followed by one hundred zeroes) and *googolplex* (the numeral one followed by googol zeros) were invented in 1920 by Milton Sirotta, the nine-year-old nephew of the mathematician Edward Kasner.

There isn't a googol of anything. Physicists estimate that in the observable universe, there are *only* 3.28×10^{80} elementary particles—not even close to a googol.

Your cosmic googolplex doppelganger.
There are roughly $10^{10^{70}}$ different quantum states
that all the particles of your body could be in.
If you were to traverse a universe googolplex
meters across, you would eventually exhaust all
those quantum state possibilities and, sooner or
later, run into an exact copy of yourself.

A googol and a googolplex are unfathomably
large numbers, but when you're counting, they
are no closer to infinity than the number one.

Principa Mathematica, a seminal three-volume work on the foundation of mathematics, contains a 362-page proof concluding that one plus one does indeed equal two.

Technically, the moon does not orbit Earth. The moon moves around Earth, but Earth is also moving. Both celestial bodies orbit a common point called the barycenter, about a thousand miles underground.

For that anti-gravity lift. The spacesuits for the 1969 *Apollo 11* moon landing were made by an industrial division of Playtex, the company that gave women the Cross Your Heart and 18 Hour bras. NASA still uses the aerospace division of ILC Dover (now a separate company) for the International Space Station spacesuits.

A **bridge too far.** Film actress Jane Russell was the television spokeswoman for Playtex bras throughout the 1970s and '80s. Billionaire aerospace entrepreneur and movie producer Howard Hughes had discovered her working as a receptionist in the early 1940s and cast her as the ingenue in his love-triangle western *The Outlaw*. Teaming up with engineers from his defense contracting business, Hughes created an underwire bra to "lift and separate" Russell's size 38D breasts, using a design based on bridge truss supports. Russell maintained that she tried it on but never wore the uncomfortable contraption.

Space dogs. In 1961, as Cold War tensions were ratcheting up, Soviet Premier Nikita Khrushchev and his wife, Nina, sent President John F. Kennedy and Jackie a gift: an adorable white puppy named Pushinka ("Fluffy"). Pushinka's mother was Strelka ("Little Arrow"), who spent a day aboard *Sputnik 2* on August 19, 1960, along with Belka ("Squirrel") and a host of other earthly creatures, including a grey rabbit, forty mice, two rats, several plants, houseflies, and some fungi. They were the first earthly inhabitants to go into orbit and safely return.

The beginning of the cold thaw? Pushinka hit it off with the Kennedys' Welsh terrier, Charlie, and gave birth to four pups in June 1963, eight months after the Cuban Missile Crisis. JFK jokingly referred to them as *pupniks*.

"**Last one out, please turn off the lights.**" On May 19, 1991, Soviet cosmonaut Sergei Krikalev boarded the *Soyuz TM-12* spacecraft that took him to the *Mir* space station. On December 26, 1991, the Soviet Union dissolved, fracturing into fifteen separate countries. Amid the political turmoil, no one knew what to do with Krikalev, so he just kept circling the globe. Five thousand revolutions and 311 days later, on March 25, 1992, he returned to Earth. Krikalev has been called the last Soviet citizen—he went up a Soviet and came down a Russian.

Ｍore trusty data from Russia. In a 2019 opinion poll, 70 percent of Russians approved of Josef Stalin's role in Russian history—his highest approval rating of all time. Stalin is credited with the murders of roughly nine million civilians: three million died in gulags (forced labor camps), another million or so were shot during the Great Terror, and more than five million died during the Ukraine Famine of 1930–1933. Stanford University historian Norman Naimark explains this ambivalence: many Russian families include perpetrators of these atrocities, so they just keep their mouths shut.

The Cold War cola. In 1972, Pepsi made a deal with Khrushchev to trade cola syrup for Stolichnaya vodka—and its cola became the first capitalist consumer product sold behind the Iron Curtain. The deal stood for seventeen years, but converting the ruble posed a problem, so Pepsi asked for a sweetener. President Mikhail S. Gorbachev kicked in the most fungible assets at his disposal: seventeen submarines, a cruiser, a frigate, and a destroyer. So for a few days in 1989, before quickly selling the vessels for scrap, Pepsi was the sixth-largest military in the world.

Row, row, row your submarine. Dutch inventor Cornelis Drebbel created the first navigable submarine—essentially, an underwater rowboat propelled by oar power and kept watertight by a skin of greased leather stretched over the wooden frame. It was successfully launched in the Thames River in 1620, the same year a group of separatists set sail for the New World in search of religious freedom.

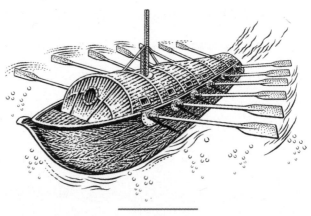

Today we call these religious separatists "the Pilgrims," but they referred to themselves as "Saints"—God's chosen people, guaranteed eternal life. They had a different name for the merchants aboard the *Mayflower*, who were seeking economic opportunity in the New World: "Strangers."

Those witches were tripping. The strange symptoms that ignited the Salem witch trials—hallucinations, incomprehensible speech, and odd skin sensations—were most likely caused by ergot poisoning from moldy rye bread. Ergot (*Claviceps purpurea*) is a fungus that infects cereal grasses like wheat and rye. It contains potent chemicals called ergot alkaloids, including lysergic acid (from which LSD is derived) and ergotamine (now used to treat migraine headaches).

Giving the devil his due. In February 2019, the IRS officially recognized the Satanic Temple as a church, meaning it has 501(c)(3) tax-exempt status. The Satanic Temple headquarters is located in a former funeral home in Salem, Massachusetts.

I **love you, man!** Just like college-aged revelers at Coachella, octopuses high on Ecstasy crave Molly hugs. Although vertebrates and invertebrates diverged over 500 million years ago, we still share the same essential neurobiology that regulates social interaction.

G**o f**k yourself!** Like the praying mantis, female octopuses are prone to sexual cannibalism. To avoid getting bumped off while bumping uglies, the male argonaut octopus detaches its specialized mating arm, called a hectocotylus, and just gives it to the female before darting away to safety.

In addition to having eight arms, octopuses have nine brains, three hearts, and blue blood. While a central brain controls the nervous system as a whole, each tentacle has its own brain that lets the limbs move independently. One heart pumps blood through the body; the other two pump blood to the gills. Hemocyanin uses copper (instead of iron) to bind with oxygen, which turns the mollusk's blood blue.

Reach out and touch someone. Relative to body size, the barnacle has the largest penis in the animal kingdom. This stationary crustacean can grow its member up to eight times the length of its body, allowing it to deposit sperm in a neighbor's shell. In some species, when breeding season is over, the appendage just falls off, only to grow again the following year.

I have to pee like a seahorse. Blue crabs mark their territory with urine—even underwater. The crab pee is a death threat to rival crustaceans: "Scat, or get scarfed."

Happy **Father's Day.** Seahorses (and their close relatives in the *Syngnathidae* family, pipefish and seadragons) are the only known animal species whose males become pregnant. Seahorses are generally monogamous, and before a mating pair invests in a pregnancy of up to six weeks, they will engage in daily greetings that involve courting dances, mutual color changes, and promenades.

Coming out of our shells. Lobsters and humans share a common ancestor dating back 350 million years. Like us, lobsters have a nervous system that deploys serotonin as a neurotransmitter—meaning Prozac, a selective serotonin reuptake inhibitor, lifts the spirits of emotionally crushed crustaceans. Pumped up on psychotropic medication, they demonstrate a renewed willingness to stand up to dominant lobsters.

You're so shellfish. The next time you're scarfing down lobster at a seafood restaurant, consider this: the modern-day lobster's ancestors were alive when *T. rex* roamed Earth, and they survived the Late Cretaceous mass extinction that wiped out the dinosaurs.

Dino-might. If the 7.5-mile-wide asteroid that killed off the dinosaurs had struck Earth thirty seconds later—and landed in the ocean—those terrifying lizards would have survived.

Hey albatross, why the long egg? In a comprehensive study of egg shapes across 1,400 bird species, scientists discovered that birds hatched from long or pointy eggs become the strongest fliers.

Some turtles can breathe through their butts. These butt-breathing turtles have the ability to stay underwater for extended periods by sucking water in through their cloacae and passing dissolved oxygen past their papillae, similarly to how fish use gills.

Though mammals cannot breathe underwater, some can smell there. Certain species of moles and shrews blow out bubbles from their noses then quickly re-inhale, sniffing the air inside the bubble for traces of underwater prey.

Naked mole rats are the only known cold-blooded mammals.

You're driving me nuts! For most mammals, maintaining a strong social network is vital for longevity. Not so for the yellow-bellied marmot, a stout ground squirrel native to the Rocky Mountains. Antisocial marmots live 13 percent longer than their gregarious counterparts.

Tusk, tusk. Tipping the scale at a whopping 14,000 pounds, the African elephant is the largest extant land mammal. Its closest relative, the rock hyrax, looks like a stubby-tailed rabbit and weighs just 14 pounds.

Hippos and blue whales are first cousins.
A DNA research study showed that hippos
and cetaceans—the order that includes whales,
porpoises, and dolphins—share a semiaquatic
mammalian ancestor some forty million
years ago.

Six hippos end-to-end are roughly the same size as one blue whale.

SPF Hippo. Hippos release a natural sunscreen. The red-colored secretion is a highly acidic complex compound sometimes referred to as "blood sweat"—although technically it is neither blood nor sweat.

Bless you. Looking at the sun makes one out of three people sneeze. Neurologists believe that the photic sneeze reflex, or "sun sneeze," is caused by crossed wires in the brain. The trigeminal nerve, which senses the irritation that causes a normal sneeze, is right next to the optic nerve. When the optic nerve gets overloaded, the electrical signal spills over and triggers a sneeze.

These slugs are *green*. *Elysia chlorotica,* a green sea slug native to the Eastern Seaboard of the United States, is the only known animal that can carry out photosynthesis. The slug's DNA contains a gene that allows it to "steal" chloroplasts from the algae it eats. Once it has enough, the slug can live off sunlight for up to nine months.

The psychedelically colored nudibranch (*Cratena peregrina*) practices "kleptopredation." That is, this sea slug prefers to eat its anemone-like prey *after* those tentacled creatures have stuffed themselves to the gills with plankton—something the nudibranch can't capture on its own.

Some bacteria can "breathe" arsenic. Found in hot springs and other environments where oxygen is scarce, these bacteria use arsenic for photosynthesis. Scientists believe this ability to process arsenic evolved billions of years ago when the planet's oceans were devoid of oxygen.

You grow, girl. Researchers in Canada have discovered that plants from the same species of beach-dwelling wildflower—known as "sea rocket"—grew aggressively alongside unrelated neighbors but were more cooperative when they shared soil with their siblings. According to the researchers, this suggests that plants, though lacking cognition and memory, are capable of complex social interactions.

Gender discrimination! According to a 2011 study, animals in biomedical research are five times more likely to be male than female.

Ant slavery. *Protomagnathus americanus* raid the colonies of other ant species, kill the adults, and steal all the larvae they can carry back to their own nest. Stolen ants assume their masters' odor and are forced to work for the slaver queen, even taking part in new raids. Rebellious ants from the genus *Temnothorax,* however, neglect and deliberately kill their captors' pupae. In such uprisings, two-thirds of the slavers' colony dies before hatching.

The spiny helmet daphnia (*Daphnia pulex*), so called because it can grow a protective headgear when it senses a nearby threat, is a tiny water flea related to the cockroach. It has at least 30,907 genes—about 8,000 more than you have.

Fleas that live on dogs jump higher and farther than fleas that live on cats.

"**Able to leap tall buildings in a single bound!**" A hungry flea in search of food can jump six hundred times an hour for three days straight, each jump the equivalent of a human being leaping over the Empire State Building.

During jumps, fleas reach peak acceleration of 150 G's—more than thirty times the gravitational force endured by astronauts during the launch of the *Saturn V* moon rocket.

Culture wars. We have about the same number of bacteria living inside us as we have human cells. In fact, the ratio is so close that one evacuation event can swing the balance, favoring bacteria over human cells or vice versa.

Hello! **I'm in here!** If you're waiting for a Danish elevator and the *i fart* button is lit up, it means the lift is occupied.

Lunch at your desk may be more hazardous than licking a toilet seat. Studies show that your office keyboard harbors four hundred times more bacteria than the toilet seat in the company bathroom. And forget about eating at a picnic table—outdoor port-o-potties are cleaner than both picnic tables and children's playground equipment.

Germs über alles. A 2014 study of German health care workers and the devices they use found that every touchscreen is contaminated with at least one organism.

It might be time for a new one. After ten years of use, your pillow is likely to acquire 50 percent of its solid weight from dead dust mites and dust mite excrement.

Oh baby! According to the Chicago Smell and Taste Treatment and Research Foundation, the combined aroma of lavender and pumpkin pie is the most potent aphrodisiac for men. For women, it's baby powder.

Whistle while you work. Studies show that men who do their share of domestic chores have more sex than their shirking counterparts.

Roses are red, my pills are blue. Drop 1 mg of a standard 50 mg dose of Viagra in a vase of cut flowers, and they will stand at attention for a week longer than usual. What you do with the other 49 mg is up to you.

Wedding frown. People who frown in photos are five times more likely to get divorced than people who smile.

The muscles in the human face can form more than fifty different smiles. New research suggests that these smiles fall into three main categories: reward, affiliation, and dominance.

A**merican cheese.** Americans smile more than people in any other country. In countries with diverse populations, smiling builds trust and cooperation and helps create social bonds between people who might not speak the same language. In more homogenous nations, smiling is an expression of social domination.

America's game. Poker gets its name from poque, a French parlor game brought to New Orleans in the early 1800s, in which four players vie for the best hand in a twenty-card deck. Traveling up and down the Mississippi River on steamboats, it eventually combined with brag, a British game that allows players to draw cards to improve their hand, and the deck was expanded to fifty-two cards so more players could sit in. Draw poker is first mentioned in print in the 1850 edition of *Bohn's New Handbook of Games*.

I **see you, and I'll raise you.** Your eyes send an electrical signal from front to back, even when you're sleeping. Scientists at the University of California, San Diego, have created robotic contact lenses that harness that electrical charge and allow you to zoom in and out by blinking twice.

When Irish eyes are smiling. In 2008, an Irishman blinded by an explosion had his sight restored after doctors inserted his son's tooth in his eye. Osteo-odonto-keratoprosthesis (OOKP), commonly referred to as "tooth in eye surgery," creates an artificial cornea by implanting a lens in a hollowed-out canine tooth. Over one hundred such operations have been performed in the U.K. since 2008, with an 80 percent success rate.

Cool as a cucumber. Cucumbers contain more water (96 percent) than watermelons (92 percent), skim milk (91 percent), or coconut water (95 percent). The cucumber's high water content keeps the inside approximately 11 degrees cooler than the external temperature, which explains the origin of the phrase *cool as a cucumber.*

Put that in your index! In 2000, *Harper's Magazine* paid a $4,000 advance to struggling writer James McManus for a piece on high-stakes gamblers. Instead of interviewing suitable subjects, McManus read a few books on Texas Hold'em, gambled the advance on a Las Vegas tournament entry fee, and miraculously won—qualifying for the $10,000 buy-in at that year's World Series of Poker. He became the first amateur ever to make the final table, finishing fifth. All told, he parlayed the *Harper's* advance into a $247,760 payday plus a book deal for *Positively Fifth Street*, which chronicles his amazing story playing America's game.

The word *scruple* derives from the Latin for "small stone." Having scruples refers to your conscience bothering you as would a pebble in your shoe.

Everybody must get. . . The use of compounds such as *stone drunk* and *stone cold* to describe a state of lifeless intoxication dates to at least 1852. These phrases referred to alcohol consumption, but the modern usage—as a single word referring to intoxication from other substances—is first recorded in *Hepcats Jive Talk Dictionary* published in 1945.

Pinocchi-uh-oh! In Carlo Collodi's beloved children's book *The Adventures of Pinocchio*, Pinocchio's nose doubles in size every time he tells a lie. Lucky for the little wooden puppet, he stops at three. Pinocchio's one-inch-long nose would grow to 341 feet after thirteen consecutive fibs, and the weight of it would snap his neck like a twig.

When you lie, your nose actually shrinks. A liar's forehead temperature rises while the temperature of the tip of the nose drops, causing shrinkage. The infrared camera technique developed by scientists at Spain's University of Granada to capture these subtle changes is more accurate than a polygraph.

"**I am a Ford, not a Lincoln.**" In 1973, Republican Vice President Spiro Agnew pleaded no contest to money laundering and tax evasion before resigning from office. President Nixon nominated Gerald Ford, then minority leader of the House of Representatives, as the first vice president to take office under the Twenty-Fifth Amendment. Less than ten months later, Nixon resigned after tape recordings were discovered of him discussing a plan to cover up the Watergate hotel break-in. Ford became president before ever stepping foot into the vice president's official residence at Number One Observatory Circle.

A **dishwatery opinion.** Though he is now considered America's greatest president, Abraham Lincoln couldn't always get a fair shake from the press—especially in his home state. In reaction to one of the nation's best-remembered political speeches, the Gettysburg Address, the Democratic-leaning *Chicago Times* reported: "The cheek of every American must tingle with shame as he reads the silly, flat, and dishwatery utterances of the man who has to be pointed out to intelligent foreigners as the president of the United States."

General George Armstrong Custer was the "goat" of the United States Military Academy at West Point in 1861. Unlike today's hyperbolic definition of the acronym—"greatest of all time"—a goat is the cadet who finishes last in his class.

Six West Point "goats" fought in the Battle of Gettysburg, including Custer, who became the youngest general in the Union army at just twenty-three years old, and Confederate General George Pickett (last in his 1846 class), whose failed charge was a decisive turning point in the Civil War.

Master of horror, but kind of a crappy cadet. Edgar Allan Poe, best remembered for being the originator of the modern detective story and a master of the macabre, was expelled from West Point in 1831 for disobedience and gross neglect of duty. He was more interested in writing poetry than studying military history.

The Raven, published by the *New York Evening Mirror* on January 29, 1845, is Poe's most famous poem. It tells the story of a young man distraught over the loss of his love and tormented by a raven that seems to have supernatural powers. Poe is the only American author with an NFL football team named in honor of his work—the Baltimore Ravens.

Flying the coop. Poe died in 1849 under mysterious circumstances after turning up delirious in a Baltimore gutter, wearing someone else's clothing. Many theories about the cause of death have been proposed, from opium and alcohol poisoning to rabies to "cooping"—when local gangs kidnapped innocent civilians and kept them in coops, beating them until they agreed to vote for a favored corrupt politician.

With 620,000 dead, the Civil War was the bloodiest war in American history. Around the same time in China, a Christian convert named Hong Xiuquan led a revolt to eradicate Confucianism, Buddhism, and folk religions and replace them with a Christian utopia he called the Taiping Heavenly Kingdom. The Taiping Rebellion was eventually put down—but only after an estimated twenty million Chinese men, women, and children died.

The first U.S. income tax—at 3 percent on all income over $800 (roughly $22,000 today)—was enacted in 1861 to pay for the crippling costs of the Civil War. It was rescinded by Congress after the war, and later attempts to create a federal income tax were declared unconstitutional by the Supreme Court.

In 1913, Congress ratified the Sixteenth Amendment and paved the way for a federal income tax to be reinstituted. Nevertheless, between fifty thousand and one hundred thousand Americans still challenge its legality each year. To deal with tax scofflaws, the IRS created the Frivolous Return Program, which it (unofficially) calls "the funny box."

The word *boycott* comes from Captain Charles Boycott, who managed the affairs of an absentee English landlord in Ireland in the late 1800s. When Boycott refused to lower the rents of his tenant farmers, the Irish Land League made an example of him by treating him like a social leper.

Do not pass go. The original Monopoly game, called the Landlord's Game, was intended as a critique of capitalism. The inventor, Lizzie Magie, was a progressive feminist and devotee of the economist Henry George, who believed a "single tax" on land value should fund all government expenditures. The board game was designed to provoke natural suspicions of unfairness about a system that enriches property owners while impoverishing tenants.

OK **Renters**. *Mortgage* literally means (in Old French) "death grip" or "death pledge." The deal "dies" when all payments are made—or when the mortgage holder can no longer make them. Modern mortgages, however, are typically amortized (you pay off a small amount of principal each month, along with the interest)—meaning they die a little bit with each payment.

At the peak of the Japanese real estate bubble in 1989, the emperor's Imperial Palace—a compound about the size of Central Park—was worth more than all the real estate in California.

The Japanese market bubble peaked on December 29, 1989, when the Nikkei stock index hit 38,987.44 on an intraday basis, and the worst bear market on record ensued. By 2002, real estate prices had dropped to approximately 1 percent of their peak values. And at the end of 2019, a full thirty years after the bubble burst, the Nikkei closed at 23,656.62—still 39 percent below the peak.

A **bit too late.** If you had invested $100 in Bitcoin when it went on the market in 2010 and then sold it in December 2017, you would've made more than $25 million.

F**unny money.** In 2018, Dogecoin—a cryptocurrency created five years earlier as a parody and named after an Internet meme—had a market value of more than $1 billion.

Compound interesting. If you'd invested one penny at the time of Christ's birth and earned 5 percent interest per year, by the time Christopher Columbus set sail in 1492 you would have had enough money to buy a ball of gold equal to the weight of Earth. At that time, the average cost of gold was about $3,000 per ounce (adjusted for inflation), and Earth weighs thirteen septillion one hundred seventy sextillion (13,170,000,000,000,000,000,000,000) pounds.

From 2010 to 2019, Amazon founder and CEO Jeff Bezos watched his net worth balloon by roughly 31 percent each year. Already a billionaire, Bezos at this rate will become the first member of the *four* comma club by the time he's eligible for Social Security.

You're richer than you think. As of 2018, if your net worth were $4,210, you'd be richer than half of the world's population. A net worth of $93,170 would put you in the top 10 percent. Anyone worth more than $871,320 is a 1 percenter.

Keep the change. The largest denomination banknote ever in circulation was the Hungarian hundred quintillion (100,000,000,000,000,000,000) *pengő*, minted in July 1946 during the worst case of hyperinflation the world has ever seen. There were too many zeros to depict on the banknote. An even larger, one sextillion note was printed but never issued—and when hyperinflation had run its course, that note was worth about twelve U.S. cents.

At the onset of World War I, President Woodrow Wilson brought forty-eight sheep to graze on the White House lawns in order to save the expense of mowing the expansive grounds. He even auctioned off their wool, raising $52,823 (roughly $1.35 million in 2019 dollars), which was donated to the Red Cross.

Until 1912, mail was delivered in the U.S. seven days a week. As the postal service grew in popularity in the 1800s and the local mailroom started to double as a gathering place, religious leaders noticed a decline in church attendance. Men would arrive to collect their mail, then stay on to drink and play cards. When new technologies such as trains, telegraphs, telephones, and automobiles reduced the need for daily mail, church leaders joined forces with organized labor to put an end to Sunday mail service.

Since 2007, the U.S. Postal Service has photographed every piece of mail to flow through its system and, on occasion, has turned over that information to law enforcement agencies as part of a criminal case.

Maybe the check isn't in the mail. From 2007 to 2019, the U.S. Postal Service lost $77 billion dollars. It has unfunded liabilities in excess of $120 billion. The USPS employs nearly half a million full-time employees.

Trigger warning. The phrase *basket case* was introduced into common parlance after World War I. Persistent rumors of quadruple-amputee soldiers who had to be wheeled around in basket carriages were finally put to rest when the surgeon general of the U.S. Army publicly declared, "I have personally examined the records and am able to say that there is not a single basket case . . . on this side of the water."

There was, in fact, one quadruple-amputee serviceman on this side of the water: Ethelbert "Curley" Christian, a black Canadian soldier originally from Pennsylvania, who lost all four limbs when gangrene set into his wounds. After the war, the Prince of Wales visited Christian in a Toronto hospital. This encounter lit a spark in Dalton Trumbo's imagination and became the basis for his 1938 antiwar novel *Johnny Got His Gun*.

Bang your head. The 1971 film adaptation of *Johnny Got His Gun* was the inspiration for Metallica's frenzied opus "One" and its accompanying music video. In 1989, "One" became the first heavy metal song to win a Grammy.

Tour 'em all. In 2013, Metallica became the first band to play on all seven continents. The heavy metal rockers played an unplugged concert in Antarctica, with audience members listening to the show through headphones to avoid disturbing the delicate setting.

Guitar legend Eric Clapton grew up believing his mother was his older sister. So did Academy Award–winning actor Jack Nicholson.

The words *rocking* and *rolling* originated as African American euphemisms for sex in the early twentieth century, as did the term *nitty-gritty*. When radio deejay Alan Freed named the music he played on his show "rock and roll," it was partly to see how much he could get away with vis-à-vis the FCC.

Walking the line. On New Year's Day 1959, Johnny Cash played a concert at San Quentin State Prison in California. Twenty-one-year-old Merle Haggard was in the audience that night—a troubled youth serving a three-year stretch for burglary and attempted escape.

A new species of tarantula was identified in 2015 near California's Folsom Prison, immortalized in Johnny Cash's 1955 hit song "Folsom Prison Blues." Mature males are black, so the name selected—*Aphonopelma johnnycashi*, in honor of the Man in Black—seems fitting.

Paroled in 1960, Haggard went on to record thirty-eight No. 1 hits, including "Mama Tried"—a semiautobiographical song about a rebellious young man who turns twenty-one in prison—which the Grateful Dead covered at Woodstock. The influential country music singer was officially pardoned in 1972 by then-California governor Ronald Reagan.

Elephants can't jump. But they can hear with their feet.

Cats can hydrate on seawater.

Giraffe meat is kosher. A giraffe chews its cud, has cloven hooves, and produces milk that clots.

The zyzzyva is a tropical American weevil and, as of 2017, the last entry in the *Oxford English Dictionary*.

As if they weren't frightening enough . . . Crocodiles can climb trees.

Can't imagine why no one lives here. Off the Brazilian coast, just ninety miles from São Paulo, is a tiny, unpopulated island called Ilha da Queimada Grande. Locals estimate that between one and five golden lanceheads—ultra-venomous pit vipers that can grow up to a foot and a half in length—inhabit every ten square feet. Unless you're a migratory bird (the vipers' primary meal), the Brazilian Navy expressly forbids landing on "Snake Island."

The Amazon River dumps the equivalent of eighty-eight Olympic-sized pools of water into the Atlantic Ocean every second. The river plume flows with such force that sailors two hundred miles out to sea can drink its fresh water.

The Amazon is the largest river in the world. No bridges cross it.

The endless wave. Every February and March, surfers gather along the Amazon to ride the *Pororoca*, a massive tidal bore wave the locals call "the great destructive noise." When the moon, the sun, and Earth fall into direct alignment, their combined gravitational pull funnels the Atlantic Ocean into the Amazon River basin. Twelve-foot swells race hundreds of miles upstream at 20 mph. A record-setting ride on this "Amazonian tsunami" lasted more than half an hour over a span of seven miles.

Don't get it twisted. The Corlios force is an effect that twists air masses and ocean currents into a spiral as they move away from the equator. In the Northern Hemisphere, these cyclonic systems turn counterclockwise; in the Southern Hemisphere, they turn clockwise. But the Corlios force is only measurable across great distances and over long periods of time. Anyone who says toilets flush in different directions according to hemisphere has got it twisted.

The phrase *the bitter end* is a nautical term referring to the "bitt" around which a cable or rope is wound. If a rope is played out to the bitter's end, the anchor has likely hit the sea floor and you are out of line.

The phrase *beat the rush* was coined in reference to the USRC *Richard Rush*, a United States Revenue Cutter Service ship tasked with law enforcement and tax collection in the Alaskan waters in the mid-1800s. Local black marketeers would race to sell undeclared seal pelts before the ship docked, thereby beating the *Rush*.

Tick the bucket. Dave Freeman, coauthor of the travel guide *100 Things to Do Before You Die*, managed to tick only fifty items off his best-selling bucket list before dying in an accident at age forty-seven.

Why **I oughta . . .** The phrase *smart aleck* comes from Alec Hoag—an infamous pimp, thief, and fraudster operating in New York City in the 1840s. With the help of some prostitutes and a few cops on the take, Hoag ran a con called the "panel game," entering the brothel through a secret panel to fleece unsuspecting johns. Hoag earned the nickname "smart Alec" when the cops busted him for cutting them out of the action.

Long-term bondage. New York City still pays 7 percent interest on bonds issued in 1873 to fund an access road to a racetrack in the Bronx. Jerome Park—home of the first Belmont Stakes—and the road leading to it were the brainchild of Leonard W. Jerome, Winston Churchill's grandfather. Some of the bonds were sold with a 274-year final maturity and don't come due until 2147.

Teddy Roosevelt saved football and helped found the NCAA. When eighteen football players died on the field during the 1905 season, the public clamored for a ban on the sport. An ardent fan, President Roosevelt used the bully pulpit to institute rules outlawing dirty play and excessive brutality. The new rules also introduced the forward pass and set the first down at ten yards instead of five. Roosevelt's involvement led to the formation of a stronger governing body, the Intercollegiate Athletic Association, which later became the NCAA.

Bully! When enlisting in 1898, ten of the Rough Riders—the volunteer cavalry unit that fought with Teddy Roosevelt in Cuba during the Spanish-American War—wrote *football player* in the space provided for occupation.

Hail **Mary.** U.S. Air Force research laboratory documents testify to a theoretical nonlethal chemical weapon informally known as the "gay bomb" or "poof bomb." The reports, which acknowledge that currently there are no known chemicals to cause homosexual behavior, also propose a chemical weapon that would give the enemy bad breath, a "heavy sweating bomb," and a "flatulence bomb"—all of which would allow Americans to sniff out combatants (and would be fairly damaging to enemy morale, too).

With allies like this, who needs enemies? On March 1, 2007, Switzerland invaded Liechtenstein when 170 soldiers from the neutral nation accidentally *blitzkrieged* their way over the tiny principality's unmarked border. The Swiss troops quickly turned back when they realized their mistake. An interior ministry spokesman from Liechtenstein said no one had even noticed.

This was not the first Swiss "attack" on Liechtenstein, which, incidentally, hasn't had an army since 1868. In 1968, Swiss soldiers accidentally bombed Malbun, the microstate's only ski resort, when a live ammunition exercise went awry—destroying some pretty good deck chairs in the process.

Hot cocoa, anyone? At Ski Dubai, one of the largest indoor ski resorts in the world, an insulation system keeps the temperature just below freezing. Meanwhile, the desert beyond its walls burns beyond 120°F.

The builders of the Els Club golf course at Dubai Sports City imported sand from Saudi Arabia for the sand traps. Although Dubai lies within the Arabian Desert, its sand is too symmetrical. Properly frustrating sand traps require angular grains of sand so that golf balls roll to the bottom of the bunker rather than lodge in its banks.

Text ya later. Under Islamic Sharia law, a man can divorce his wife simply by saying the word *talaq* ("I divorce you") three times. Triple Talaq, as this practice is widely known, now extends to both emails and text messages, as long as they are clear and unambiguous. Some countries are pushing back on this, however. In 2019, India made Triple Talaq a criminal offense, punishable by up to three years in jail.

In early 2019, Sultan Muhammad V of Malaysia abdicated his throne to marry Oksana Voevodina, a Russian model and former Miss Moscow. Six months later, he divorced her by a Triple Talaq text message. When the press asked about the abrupt ending of her storybook romance, the ex-beauty queen claimed for months that she was unaware of any such divorce and continued to post happy family pictures on Instagram. Status update: it's over.

Sins of the forefathers? Published in 1830, *The Life of Mohammed* was the first American biography about the founder of Islam. It describes Mohammed as an "imposter" and calls Islam a "heresy" and a "horrid superstition." The author was biblical scholar George Bush (1796–1859)—a distant relative of the two conservative presidents who waged wars in the Middle East.

According to BabyCenter, a parenting website, in 2019 Muhammad entered the list of the top ten most popular baby names for boys in the United States.

"**I want my zombie!**" Newborns typically deprive their parents of 350 to 400 hours of sleep in the first year.

Sleep tight. Created in 1849, Mrs. Winslow's Soothing Syrup was marketed as a cure-all for fussy babies. Because this was before the Pure Food and Drug Act of 1906, the manufacturer was not required to disclose the two primary ingredients: morphine and alcohol. One teaspoon contained 65 mg of morphine, which led to the medicine's unfortunate nickname: "the baby killer."

Dirt is good for you. As any toddler knows instinctively, eating or playing in dirt (which contains myriad bacteria) helps boost fledgling immune systems. The five-second rule is a myth—microbes can attach themselves to a dropped food particle in milliseconds—but unless you've dropped your morsel in a known pathogen, living by the "rule" is harmless.

There is no word for "Buddhism" in Buddhism. Nineteenth-century English translators added the Greek suffix -ism, meaning doctrine, to Buddha's name, but he used the term *marga* to describe the Eightfold Path to enlightenment.

The *Jikji*, a collection of Zen Buddhist teachings, is the oldest book printed using metal movable type. It was published by Korean monks in 1377—seventy-eight years before Johannes Gutenberg started cranking out Bibles in Mainz, Germany.

The first book Gutenberg published was not the Bible. It was a twenty-eight-page section from the *Ars Grammatica*, a dour primer on Latin grammar, published sometime around 1450. Gutenberg later decided to publish the Bible because he was looking for a best seller.

The fine print. Gutenberg didn't make a dime selling his Bibles. He lost a lawsuit brought by his partner, Johann Fust, and was financially ruined.

The Bible is . . . inconsistent. According to the Book of Leviticus, shaving one's beard is a sin. Getting a tattoo or wearing a cotton-poly T-shirt (or any garment of mixed fiber) will likewise incur God's wrath.

Whack job. In 1642, the Pilgrims declared seventeen-year-old Thomas Granger guilty of having impure relations with a horse, a cow, two calves, two goats, five sheep, and a turkey. As per Leviticus 20:15, they made him watch the slaughter of the animals before executing him.

The **Lord's player.** In 1631, royal printers Robert Barker and Martin Lucas published a King James Bible with a couple of egregious errors. The "Wicked Bible," as it has become known, left the word *not* out of the seventh commandment so that it reads, "Thou shalt commit adultery." A second erratum produced "our God hath shewed us his glory and *his great asse*" instead of *"his greatness"* (Deuteronomy 5:24).

Barker and Lucas were fined £300 (the equivalent of about $60,000 in today's dollars) and were prohibited from printing Bibles. All but eleven copies of the one thousand Wicked Bibles were destroyed. In 2015, one of them sold at auction for roughly $40,000.

The Game and Playe of the Chesse, a book about morality that uses chess as a metaphor, was the first English-language book published in England. The very first book in English, *The Recuyell of the Histories of Troy*—a collection of stories loosely based on tales of the Trojan War—was published in Belgium a year earlier, in 1473.

Scat Cats. In Spain, Catalans have a scatological take on the traditional Christmas Yule log. Children with sticks whack the *Caga Tió*—a log painted with a broad, smiling face and covered with a blanket—while singing, "*Caga, tió, caga!*" ("Crap, log, crap!") If the children have been good, parents reach under the blanket to dole out "crap" in the form of candy, nuts, and nougat.

In Barcelona, Catalonia's capital city, nativity scenes lodge an unexpected figurine alongside the animals, the magi, Mary and Joseph, and the baby Jesus: the *caganer* ("crapper"), a gnome-like creature in a red hat squatting over a cone of excrement. In recent years, the tradition has been extended to include American political figures like Barack Obama, Hillary Clinton, and Donald Trump in the crapper position.

There are two talking animals in the Old Testament: the serpent in the Garden of Eden (Genesis) and Balaam's talking ass (Numbers).

Common names were the first keywords. The onager (*Equus hermionus*), a central Asian species that belongs to the horse family, is commonly referred to as the "Asian wild ass" and the "half ass."

The American usage of *half-assed* to mean "ineffectual" or "unplanned" dates back to 1932 and may derive from a playful mispronunciation of *haphazard.*

Sounds fishy. At over four feet long and weighing more than a hundred pounds, the South American capybara is the largest rodent in the world. Sometime between the sixteenth and eighteenth centuries, the Catholic Church classified it as a "fish" so it could be eaten during Lent.

Saint Patrick may be the patron saint of Ireland, but he was born a Roman citizen of Britain.

The word *arena* is Latin for "dust" or "sand." The floors of arenas—most famously, Rome's Colosseum—were covered in sand to soak up spilled blood so that gladiators fighting for their lives wouldn't slip.

When Julius Caesar brought the first giraffe to Europe in 46 BCE, Romans called it a "camelopard." Years after its remarkable debut at the Circus Maximus chariot races, some of these docile creatures were displayed in the Colosseum, where lions tore them to shreds.

A wolf in sheep's clothing is an idiomatic expression describing someone who hides malicious intent under a harmless disguise. Its first known usage is in the fourth-century *Codex Sinaiticus* (or "Sinai Bible"), handwritten in Greek and the oldest complete copy of the New Testament. It's from Matthew 7:15: "Beware of false prophets, who come to you in sheep's clothing, but within are ravenous wolves."

This place is a zoo! Built by King Philip Augustus in 1190, the Louvre—the world's largest art museum, located in the center of Paris—was originally a *louvèterie*, the kennel of a wolf-hunting guild (derived from the Old French *louvet*, meaning "wolf pup").

Art makes us kinder. According to a massive study in the U.K. conducted by the Economic and Social Research Council, making art and attending performances are the two strongest predictors of charitable giving and working as a volunteer.

In 2017, a grasshopper was found embedded in a 128-year-old painting by Vincent van Gogh. In a letter to his brother, Van Gogh kvetched about how frustrating painting *en plein air* could be: "I must have picked up a good hundred flies and more off the four canvases that you'll be getting, not to mention dust and sand."

Warm hands, warm heart. Studies of blood flow in the brain show a direct link between physical and emotional warmth. Holding something warm can make you feel more generous and trusting toward others, while holding something cold makes you more feel more isolated and judgmental.

Meet your Waterloo. Trying new things is hard, but often rewarding. A two-day London Underground strike in 2014 forced commuters to find alternate routes. When service was restored, one in twenty Londoners stuck to their new route—having shaved an average seven minutes off their commute.

The most ubiquitous typeface in history, Times New Roman, came about as a result of a damning letter to the editor back in 1929. After criticizing the British *Times* for being badly printed and old-fashioned, type designer Stanley Morison was commissioned by the newspaper to create the serif typeface.

Talk nerdy to me. What did amorous Italian spy Giacomo Casanova, author Jacob Grimm, American founding father Benjamin Franklin, French conceptual artist Marcel Duchamp, former Israeli prime minister Golda Meir, FBI founder and director J. Edgar Hoover, and revolutionary hero and Communist dictator Mao Zedong have in common? They were all librarians.

Dr. Seuss invented the word *nerd* for his 1950 children's book *If I Ran the Zoo.*

The Dewey Decimal System has been adopted all over the world. It organizes library contents into ten groups, each assigned with one hundred subcategories. Over the years, Dewey's system has been revised to overcome his racial, gender, and religious biases.

Dewey Hatem & Howe. In 2019, the American Library Association (ALA) decided to rename the Melvil Dewey award. The disgraced co-founder of the ALA sexually harassed four women in 1905 and was forced to step down the following year.

Pishposh. There's a rule for pairing words with internal vowel alternations: it's called ablaut reduplication. Sounds you make high in your mouth always come before sounds you make low in your mouth, so *I* comes before either *A* or *O*. And if there are three words in succession ("bish-bash-bosh," as the Brits say when they efficiently wrap up a task), then the order is always *I*, *A*, *O*.

A **language dies every two weeks.** There were 7,111 active languages being spoken in 2019. Forty percent are presently endangered—less than a thousand people speak them—and linguists believe half will disappear before the end of the century. Just twenty-three languages are used by half the world's population.

Egghead? The coded information in the chromosomes of a single fertilized human egg contains the equivalent of roughly one thousand printed volumes of books, each as large as a volume of the *Encyclopedia Britannica*.

The 2010 version of the *Encyclopedia Britannica*, published in thirty-two volumes, was the final printed edition. Counting only the English-language pages, Wikipedia in its current form would span more than 2,600 volumes of equivalent size.

Even Nobel laureates may be tempted to cheat. After it was announced that American balladeer Bob Dylan would be awarded the Nobel Prize in Literature, Dylan didn't show up to class—that is, he skipped the awards ceremony altogether. At a private event later, Dylan delivered a lecture (a requirement of the prize) that contained twenty-one instances of plagiarism from the SparkNotes article on *Moby-Dick*.

There are bowhead whales swimming off the coast of Alaska that were born before *Moby-Dick* was written in 1851.

A whale of a tale. While writing *Moby-Dick* in Pittsfield, Massachusetts, Melville took inspiration from snow-covered Mount Greylock (the state's highest peak), which reminded him of a breaching whale. Now considered an American classic, the novel was a commercial failure at the time. Unable to make a living as a writer, Melville took a job as a customs officer in New York City. When he died in 1891, the book was out of print.

A "widow's walk" is an architectural feature common in nineteenth-century houses built along the Eastern Seaboard. This small, railed rooftop platform, often surrounding the chimney, supposedly was where a mariner's wife would cast her eyes toward the ocean and wait anxiously to learn whether her husband's ship would return. The platform's actual purpose, however, was to allow residents to pour sand down the chimney in case of fire.

A **room with a view.** The Taj Mahal in Agra, India, was commissioned in 1632 as a tribute to Shah Jahān's second wife, Mumtaz Mahal, who had recently died in childbirth. Shortly after its completion twenty-two years later, the Shah was deposed and imprisoned by his son, Aurangzeb, who forced his father to live out the rest of his life in a cell—one that offered a view of his majestic creation.

An otherwise typical four-story office building in Vathorst, a suburb of Amsterdam, stands out with an unexpected architectural flourish: instead of gargoyles, its brick-and-mortar facade features a gallery of twenty-two emoji.

Total SNAFU. In 2008, a construction crane in New York City collapsed, killing seven people and destroying a four-story townhouse. Among the rubble were the remains of Fubar, a tavern that had operated on the bottom floor. Often used by radiomen in World War II, FUBAR is an acronym for F$@%ed Up Beyond All Recognition.

In 2017, Pennsylvanian miners en masse turned down retraining opportunities funded by the government, choosing instead to wait for a coal comeback. In reality, the industry keeps shrinking: there are fewer miners in America than florists.

The light bulb goes on. Kentucky's coal-mining museum has installed solar panels on its roof in order to save $10,000 a year on electric costs.

Fly ash—a byproduct of coal-burning electric power plants—dumps one hundred times more radiation into the surrounding environment than a nuclear power plant producing the same amount of energy.

Bitcoin mining consumes as much energy per year as Denmark.

One unspoken consequence of climate change is the use of metaphors to describe catastrophic events. In 2017, for example, we heard that an iceberg the size of Delaware had broken away from the Antarctic Peninsula. Two years later, another iceberg calved off the Amery Ice Shelf in Antarctica, this one the size of greater Los Angeles—larger than Delaware and Rhode Island combined.

Japan's March 2011 earthquake shoved the main island of Honshu eight feet to the east.

From raging waters to Stillwater. According to the U.S. Geological Survey, the earthquake that caused the 2004 Indian Ocean tsunami—the deadliest on record—released 23,000 times more energy than the Hiroshima atomic bomb. It caused Earth to "wobble" on its axis, shortening that day by 2.68 microseconds. Shockwaves were recorded all the way in Oklahoma.

Mass communication. Digital information is stored using electrons, and electrons have mass. The entire Internet—all the websites, libraries, emails, videos, memes, social media posts, and everything else—weighs less than a can of Campbell's soup.

Some tech has royal blood. Bluetooth, a standardized protocol to wirelessly share data, gets its name from a medieval Danish king. Harald "Bluetooth" Gormsson, in addition to introducing Christianity to the Danes, united vicious tribes of Vikings—who had various dialects and customs, and who often raided each other—into a single kingdom.

Saudi Arabia was the first nation to grant citizenship to a robot.

The end times may be messier than you think. "Gray goo" is a hypothetical apocalypse scenario involving nanotechnology, in which infinitesimal robots gone haywire consume all matter on Earth while continuously replicating themselves.

Cowabunga! In 2008, the Food and Drug Administration declared that meat and milk from cloned animals and their progeny are "as safe to eat as food from conventionally bred animals."

I just threw up in my mouth a little bit. "Pink slime," or boneless lean beef trimmings (BLBT), is what's left of the cow after the butcher has removed its choice cuts. Banned in the U.K. except in dog and chicken food, this beef by-product remains legal for human consumption in the United States. To kill off bacteria such as *E. coli*, some American fast-food restaurants spray BLBT with ammonium hydroxide before shaping it into burgers, although both McDonald's and Burger King have cut it from the menu.

Root causes. The healthy vegetables your grandmother told you to eat are no longer sold in grocery stores. As a result of soil depletion (as well as the trade-offs agribusinesses make between yield levels and nutrition content), the average vegetable found in American supermarkets today is anywhere from 5 percent to 40 percent lower in minerals and nutrients than those harvested fifty years ago.

A study of American two-year-olds found that although most could not yet recognize the letter *M*, the tykes could definitely ID the Golden Arches.

Some big (red) shoes to fill. Only eight actors have served as the McDonald's mascot. More men have walked on the moon than have portrayed Ronald McDonald.

In the early 1960s, founer Ray Kroc thought the McDonald's logo needed a reboot, so he hired clinical psychologist and marketing innovator Louis Cheskin as a design consultant. Cheskin convinced Kroc that the rounded *M* in the Golden Arches symbolizes a mother's mammaries. Kroc kept the logo, and "Give Mom a Night Off" became a successful advertising campaign.

The word *yahoo,* meaning a "brute in human form," comes from Jonathan Swift's 1726 satire *Gulliver's Travels.* The Yahoos eschewed reason for the sake of vice and materialism.

Boone-doggle. American frontiersman Daniel Boone often made reference to events in *Gulliver's Travels,* and even claimed that he had killed one of the hairy giants that Swift called Yahoos. Boone's tale may not be the source of the Bigfoot legend, but he played a role in popularizing it.

Pirates helped bring democracy to America. During the Golden Age of Piracy (1650–1730), everyone aboard the ship was held to a strict code of conduct, even the captain. Only a few written examples of this code survived— captured pirates would burn the paper trail—but Captain Bartholomew Roberts' articles on the *Royal Fortune* (1720) begin: "Every man has a vote in affairs of moment."

A person born on February 29 is called a "leapling." The celebration of a leapling's "true" birthday every four years is a plot device in Gilbert and Sullivan's comic operetta *The Pirates of Penzance.*

Hooray for . . . In 1886, the Midwestern pioneers Harvey and Daeida Wilcox subdivided their 120-acre ranch in southern California and began creating a community based on sober religious principles. A trip back to Ohio yielded suitable homesteading recruits and inspired a new name for their Christian paradise: Hollywood.

Marlene Dietrich, the gender norm–bashing German actress who started out as a drag king in 1920s Berlin, shared the first lesbian kiss in a Hollywood film. In Paramount Pictures' 1930 production of *Morocco*, she reprises her role as a cabaret singer. Dressed in a top hat, a white tie, and tails, her character plants one on an unsuspecting woman as Gary Cooper, the dashing love interest, swoons.

A **honeypot plot.** Despite having denounced Nazism and becoming a U.S. citizen, during World War II Marlene Dietrich offered to make a film in Germany—but only as a ploy to seduce and assassinate Adolph Hitler.

Between the years 1933 and 1945, the Nazis arrested around 100,000 men for being homosexual—5,000 to 15,000 of whom ended up in concentration camps. When the Allied forces swept through Europe liberating the camps, some gay survivors were detained and forced to serve out their original jail sentence.

In the early 1920s, the United States used Zyklon B to disinfect immigrants and day workers crossing the border from Mexico. A few years later, the Nazis used Zyklon B as the killing agent in the gas chambers.

The fundamental research for Zyklon B (a brand name for hydrogen cyanide, a lethal pesticide) was done by Fritz Haber, a 1918 Nobel Prize-winning German Jewish chemist. In one of history's most tragic ironies, Haber's work led to the death of millions of Jews, including his own extended family.

Style over substance. Isadora Duncan—the revolutionary dancer who famously dressed in billowing silks and stylish, toga-like drapery— met an untimely death in 1927 when her long, flowing scarf got caught in the rear axle of a convertible sportscar. When the poet Gertrude Stein heard the news, she reportedly said, "Affectations can be dangerous."

Put it on the Liszt. John Williams, who composed the memorable scores for *Star Wars*, *Indiana Jones*, *Jaws*, *Jurassic Park*, and other blockbusters, has never watched a single *Star Wars* film.

Raise a glass to freedom. Williams didn't compose *all* the music in the *Star Wars* films. The cantina stomp featured in *Star Wars: The Force Awakens*, dubbed "Jabba Flow," was co-written by the director J. J. Abrams and Lin-Manuel Miranda, the maestro behind the hip-hop Broadway musical *Hamilton*.

A few years after killing founding father Alexander Hamilton in a duel, Aaron Burr tried to steal Louisiana Purchase land in an attempt to crown himself Emperor of Mexico. He was acquitted of treason, but to escape the nation's enmity (and his creditors), Burr fled to Europe—where he tried to convince Napoléon Bonaparte, Emperor of France, to conquer Florida.

In 1776, American colonists earned higher wages and paid lower taxes than British citizens living in Great Britain. "No taxation without representation"—the grievance that gave rise to the American Revolution—was based on principle, not burden.

America's first fireworks-studded celebration of the Fourth of July occurred in Philadelphia in 1777—one year after the signing of the Declaration of Independence and a full six years before the end of the Revolutionary War. Historians believe the celebration was intended to boost morale.

Not all chairs are created equal. Thomas Jefferson was a lifelong inventor, maker, and tinkerer. He wrote the Declaration of Independence while sitting in a revolving comb-back Windsor chair built to his design specifications.

Phuket, man. America may call itself the land of the free—the phrase is in the national anthem—but the word *Thailand* literally means "land of the free." *Thai* means "free man" or "human being."

The King and I (both musical and film versions) is banned in Thailand, but Anna Leonowens' memoir, *The English Governess at the Siamese Court* (1870)—about tutoring King Mongkut's thirty-two wives and concubines and eighty-two children—is still in print. A new Thai translation came out in 2019.

Croatia means "tie-land." *Hrvat*, the Croatian word for "Croat," is also the origin of *cravat*, the forerunner of our modern tie. Croatian mercenaries wearing neck cloths brought their military style to Paris in the 1630s when King Louis XIII enlisted them to support his power struggle against his own mother, Marie de Medici.

In the mid-1700s, the flowing cravat was re-introduced by the British "macaroni." Young aristocrats returned from their Grand Tour of continental Europe with a penchant for pasta and an over-the-top, gender-nonconforming style that included tall, effeminate wigs; tight-fitting clothing; and the aforementioned cravat. Anything that was in fashion was said to be "macaroni."

Don't hate on my style. In the song "Yankee Doodle," the central figure stuck "a feather in his cap and called it macaroni." British military officers came up with this ditty to mock the disheveled, disorganized Yankees with whom they served in the French and Indian War (1754–1763). *Doodle* was seventeenth-century slang for "fool" or "simpleton"—in other words, Yankees were so dumb, they thought sticking a feather in their hat was stylish.

Thomas Jefferson didn't invent macaroni and cheese (recipes date back to fourteenth-century Italy), but he did introduce it to America. He even served it at a state dinner in 1802, a meal prepared by James Hemings—his enslaved personal chef and the brother of Sally Hemings, the mother of six of Jefferson's children.

The word *bank* comes from the Italian *banca,* meaning "bench." In fifteenth-century Venice, Christians were forbidden from lending money with interest because the Catholic Church had denounced it as a sin. Jews, who were barred from most other professions, became money-lenders and conducted their business on benches in the plaza.

The word *credit* comes from the Latin *credo,* meaning "I believe"—as in "I believe you will pay me back."

It's not me, it's you. Benito Mussolini developed revolutionary fascism in Italy with Margherita Sarfatti, his Jewish mistress and cultural advisor. Il Duce kicked Sarfatti out of his bed (and Italy) when he passed race laws in November 1938 hoping to curry favor with Hitler's Germany on the eve of World War II.

Pardon me, do you have any Grey Poupon? While on the run during the great exodus, the Jews ate foie gras. They had learned how to force-feed ducks and geese from their Egyptian oppressors, who had been fattening fowl since 2500 BCE.

Only 3 percent of bird species have a functioning penis—a group that includes ducks, ostriches, and kiwis. All birds start off with an embryonic penile structure, but the BMP4 gene programs those cells to die off and wither away.

Fowl play. Male waterfowl are notorious "rapists." To combat their nonconsensual advances, some female ducks and geese have evolved faux vaginas that can twist in the opposite direction of the male's spiral phallus. Other fugazi vajay-jays collect the sperm of unwanted suitors in several "dead end" pockets.

An outgoing politician whose successor has already been elected is called a "lame duck." Stock traders in the mid-eighteenth century coined the phrase to describe anyone who couldn't pay their debts.

Genetically speaking, the duck-billed platypus is an evolutionary missing link. The egg-laying monotreme is classified as a mammal—it has fur, lactates, and suckles its young—but its genome contains DNA found only in birds and reptiles.

What the duck? When the first platypus skin and artist's sketch arrived at the British Natural History Museum in 1798, zoologist George Shaw thought he might be the victim of a hoax. He examined the cheeks for stitches, convinced that a duck's bill had been attached to a mole's body in "some deceptive preparation by artificial means."

Birds-of-paradise flaunt the blackest black in nature. On a nano scale, their super-black plumage works differently from a typical black feather. Specifically, the barbules (infinitesimal quills that branch off larger barbs) curve upward rather than lie flat. Instead of getting reflected, light bounces between the vertical barbules until it's completely absorbed.

Gaming the system. A lot of wildlife photos aren't shot in the wild. Game farms, home to captive wolves, wild cats, and bears, charge photographers hundreds of dollars per hour to stage shots that accompany articles, which then get shared and viewed countless times. According to veteran wildlife photographer Tom Mangelsen, "People fudge the captions."

The father, the clone, and the holy fish. Using a process called androgenesis, the male *Squalius alburnoides* (a Spanish river fish) is able to produce a clone of itself. Among vertebrates, it's the only known occurrence of males reproducing without females.

Mass wedding, anyone? If you eat sushi in the United States, you are indirectly supporting Sun Myung Moon's Unification Church, infamous for its Moonie mass weddings. Reverend Moon laid out his plans to become "king of the ocean" in his 1980 speech "The Way of the Tuna." Through an umbrella company called True World Group, Moon's church owns fishing boats and distribution centers, and supplies most of the nation's four thousand sushi restaurants.

File under "super-nasty." Swedish people eat *Surströmming*—fermented (literally, "soured") herring. Norwegians eat *Lutefisk*—cod soaked in lye. Icelanders eat *Hákar*—shark that has been buried in gravel for up to six months. To chase down these fetid feasts, many Scandinavians drink aquavit, from the Latin *aqua vitae*, meaning "water of life."

Aquavit is a distilled spirit infused with car-away, which has been used as a digestive aid for millennia. It is first mentioned in the Ebers Papyrus, an Egyptian medical scroll dating back to 1550 BCE.

Popping beefs in Shrewsbury. In Shakespeare's *Henry IV, Part 2*, the charismatic Falstaff—a dissolute knight who pals around with the king's son, the future Henry V—is offered baked apples with caraway to alleviate his gassy indigestion after a night of debauchery.

Back in 2008, Televen, a private Venezuelan television station, was forced to remove *The Simpsons* from its morning programming because the government deemed the show "inappropriate" for children. The station replaced the animated satire with reruns of *Baywatch*.

Wacky tomacky. In an episode of *The Simpsons* titled "E-I-E-I-D'oh" and inspired by a 1959 *Scientific American* article, Homer accidentally creates "tomacco"—a highly addictive tomato-tobacco hybrid—when he fertilizes his fields with plutonium. Longtime *Simpsons* fan Rob Baur cultivated real tomacco in 2003 and gave one of his Frankenfruits (tomatoes are fruits) to episode writer Ian Maxtone-Graham, who devoured it.

Popeye the 'roid-rage man. It turns out Popeye was onto something. Spinach contains ecdysterone, a naturally occurring hormone. During a recent study in Germany, men who were given daily supplements equivalent to eating 9 pounds of spinach showed a 300 percent spike in strength compared with the placebo group. The German researchers recommend adding ecdysterone to the World Anti-Doping Authority's list of banned substances.

In the early 1960s, a big lug of a side character was introduced to the *Popeye* comic strip: Dufus Jones. By the late 1960s, the word *doofus* caught on as someone who is slow, dimwitted, or stupid.

Nicotine occurs naturally in plants from the *Solanaceae* family, such as potatoes, tomatoes, and eggplant. But you'd have to eat 22 pounds of eggplant to consume the nicotine equivalent of one cigarette.

Oktoberfest was originally held to finish up the dregs of *Märzen,* or "March beer." Extra alcohol was added so the brew, stored in caves, would last through the summer. *Lager* is the German word for "locker" or "storage."

The three preeminent brewers in modern American history all married into the business. Joseph Schlitz, Frederick Pabst, and Adolphus Busch took over the unprofitable breweries owned by their respective fathers-in-law (the latter joined his surname to his wife's: Anheuser) and turned them into an entire industry.

Bug juice. Some strawberry yogurts and cranberry juices get their deep red coloring from ground-up bugs. The food coloring agents carmine, carminic acid, and cochineal extract are all derived from the crushed carcasses of the female *Dactylopius coccus*, a Central and South American insect that feasts on the red berries of the *Opuntia* cactus.

Marketed as a "smooth-drinking whiskey," Southern Comfort, until 2017, had contained no whiskey whatsoever for forty years.

Casu marzu is a Sardinian delicacy known colloquially as "maggot cheese." It's basically pecorino fermented to near-decomposition by the introduction of cheese fly larvae (*Piphila casei*), lending a soft texture with seeping liquid called *lagrima* (Sardinian for "tears"). People munching the cheese must protect their eyes from the maggots, which can launch themselves up to six inches. Those too squeamish to consume live maggots seal an opened cheese round in a paper sack—and when the "popcorn" sound of suffocating maggots leaping against the bag stops, the cheese is ready to enjoy.

That's some killer cheese. Ingesting *casu marzu* carries the risk of an intestinal larval infection, whose symptoms include nausea, vomiting, abdominal pain, and bloody diarrhea. Additionally, the larvae attempt to bore through internal organs with powerful mouthhooks that can lacerate stomach linings or intestinal walls. Although the Sardinian government has outlawed the cheese, one can obtain it on the black market—for twice the price of pecorino.

Seal the deal with a meal. According to a joint social psychology and business marketing study, sitting down to a meal together makes people feel closer to one another. And if you really need to seal an important deal, dine family-style. Sharing food from a common plate leads to cooperation and better negotiations.

Data from the Bureau of Labor Statistics indicates that 80 percent of small businesses survive the first year, 70 percent make it through year two, and 50 percent make it to year five. Only 30 percent are still in business after a decade.

Plan to scrap plan A. In his study of entrepreneurs, *The Origin and Evolution of New Businesses*, economist Amar Bhidé notes that 93 percent of businesses that have become successful did so only when they abandoned their original strategy.

In a paper titled "Mirror, Mirror on the Wall: The Effect of Time Spent Grooming on Wages," economists Jayoti Das and Stephen DeLoach conclude that for every extra ten minutes spent grooming each day, men can increase their weekly wages by 6 percent. For women to receive a commensurate bump, unfortunately, they would have to quadruple their daily grooming time.

This might blow your mind (not that you'd notice). Nearly all (99.999996 percent) of the information that enters your brain every second is processed unconsciously.

We are all fatheads. The human brain is nearly 60 percent fat. It's the fattiest organ in your body.

Well, this is awkward. In 2015, a New Jersey woman took a court-ordered DNA paternity test and discovered that her twin girls had different fathers. The judge ruled that the plaintiff would have to pay child support for only one of the girls.

*H*eteropaternal superfecundation means "different fathers, multiple fertilizations." In order for this to happen, a woman has to release two eggs in the same month, then have sex with two different partners within forty-eight hours. Although bipaternal twins are common among cats and dogs, it is exceedingly rare in humans—fewer than a dozen cases are on record.

Why can't you be more like your brother?
Hercules has a bipaternal twin brother named Iphicles. Zeus tricks Alcmene, Hercules's mother, by pretending to be her husband, Amphitryon, who returns from a long journey the following night. Hercules is born a god, while Iphicles is a mere mortal.

The only thing left in the box after Pandora opened it was hope.

Liquid gold. In the first century CE, two Roman emperors—Nero and Vespasian—levied a tax on urine (*vectigal urinae*), a valuable raw commodity used in toothpaste and bleach. The lower classes would dump their urine into large public cesspools, and well-off tradespeople paid the consumption tax. The funds were used to expand the Cloaca Maxima ("great sewer") system, an architectural marvel that still drains rainwater and debris away from the city of Rome.

In 2018, NYC's sewer system overflowed, on average, once every three days.

Pecunia non olet! (**"Money doesn't stink!"**) When Emperor Vespasian's son Titus expressed disgust at the dirty business of making money from bodily waste, Vespasian held a coin in front of his son's nose. Titus admitted it did not smell, and the emperor quipped, "Yet it comes from urine."

Gold coins might not smell, but paper currency does. Lab studies show that U.S. dollar bills emit a detectable fingerprint of volatile organic compounds (VOCs) that include cotton, ink, soap, leather, metal, human sweat, fecal matter, and a whole host of bacteria. Some 80 percent of U.S. bills also test positive for cocaine residue.

Mexican drug lord Joaquín "El Chapo" Guzmán Loera has twice escaped maximum-security prisons—in 2001 and 2015—and is said to be worth $1 billion. In between his daring escapes, he thanked U.S. politicians for keeping drugs illegal. He is reported to have said, "I couldn't have gotten so stinking rich without George Bush, George Bush Jr., Ronald Reagan, even El Presidente Obama. None of them have the *cojones* to stand up to all the big money that wants to keep this stuff illegal. From the bottom of my heart, I want to say: *Gracias, amigos.* I owe my whole empire to you."

Our revenue targets are . . . far out, man. Colorado legalized recreational marijuana use in 2014. Within five years, the state's coffers had increased by more than $1 billion in tax revenue from selling pot.

Up, with a twist—and a little dirty. A marijuana dispensary employee who advises customers on the myriad strains of weed and consumable products—as well as the associated laws and health concerns –is called a *budtender*, a portmanteau of "bud" and "bartender."

The first forensic laboratory devoted to linking suspects to crime scenes was established at Scotland Yard in 1901. Since that time, it has never been definitively proven that every person's fingerprints are unique.

It's go time. Death is a systemic definition—that is, it occurs when the 32.7 trillion cells in your body stop working together. But around 1 percent of your genes activate hours and sometimes days *after* you die. Scientists are not sure why these "zombie" genes express themselves, but calculating their postmortem activation may help forensics experts determine time of death.

About the Authors. Harry Bright and Jakob Anser take great pleasure in regaling each other with bizarre factoids. The pair has been known to hold forth at cocktail parties to the distraction and bemusement of their peers. They are the authors of *That's a Fact, Jack!*, *WTF [psychology]*, and *WTF [science]*.

About the Illustrator. Michael Halbert has been working as a commercial artist for forty years. He describes his style as "pen and ink on scratchboard." His work has appeared in magazines and advertising, on product packaging, and more. He lives in St. Louis, Missouri.

Get in touch. All the details of this book have been fact-checked. If you discover an error, please contact us at **info@brighthartbooks.com**

For information about upcoming titles, please join our mailing list at brighthartbooks.com. Please also follow us on Instagram at **#brighthartbooks** and on Facebook at **Bright Hart Books.**